THIS BOOK BELONGS TO:

MERRY MEET
&
MERRY PART

A BOOK OF POEMS
BY AIMEE WOOD

1st Edition Paperback.

Copyright © 2024 by Aimee Wood.
All rights reserved.

This book, in entirety or in part, may not be reproduced for commercial use without written permission from the author; brief excerpts for reviews or commentary are allowed with proper attribution and a link to the author's website.

Cover art and design by Aimee Wood.
Public domain chapter illustrations by Ida Rentoul Outhwaite.

Independently Published by Aimee Wood.
PO Box 7303, Boulder, Colorado, 80306. USA.
www.aimeewoodworks.com

ISBN: 978-1-7344731-3-1

1 2 3 4 5 6 7 8 9 10

DEDICATION.

Beware— yet trudge that lantern on,
Let moths collect their due,
What light attracts will part come dawn,
But darkness might claim you.

CONTENTS.

CHAPBOOKS.

	PAGE
1 — Write. "A Poet All Along."	13
2 — Late. "Ways to Lose."	55
3 — Choice. "Decay or Runaway."	95
4 — Rebirth. "See by Heart."	141
5 — Lost. "Cursed and Closed."	177
6 — Chance. "Flush of Heart."	217
7 — Dream. "Call the Fairies."	255
8 — Hope. "Courage Catches."	285
9 — Age. "Timeless Timed."	321

AFTERWORDS.

Postface.	359
Acknowledgments.	361
About the Poet.	363
Other Books and Editions.	365

PREFACE.

THE POETRY.

The following common meter poems fell into my journals over three difficult years. This book was my companion; through aging and timing, luck and loss, hope and rage— all the happy tragedies of life and love. It is my guide through darker nights.

THE PATH.

I consider this book to be one long poem, gathered into nine themes, bound together as a winding path through the woods. On the opposite page is a list of nine chapters; you might choose to keep the trail I have laid out, or find your own path.

ILLUSTRATIONS.

CHAPTER ART BY:
IDA RENTOUL OUTHWAITE.

	PAGE
"Garden of Dreams," Fairyland, 1926.	12
"—And Wept Bitterly," Fairyland, 1926.	54
"As if her heart would break," The Little Green Road to Fairyland, 1922.	94
"The arms of the Fairy Queen," The Little Fairy Sister, 1923.	140
"Castaway," drawing in pen and ink, 1921.	176
"Swung to & fro," Elves and Fairies, 1916.	216
"Echo," Elves and Fairies, 1916.	254
"Fairy Beauty Scattering Stars," The Enchanted Forest, 1921.	284
"Fairy of the Snow," Elves and Fairies, 1916.	320

ARTIST.

IDA RENTOUL OUTHWAITE.
1888 — 1960

Ida shaped the way we depict and cherish fairies and elves; a hundred years later, her art and poetry hold power still. Ida's early illustrations are now public domain, and I have included a few relevant pieces in this book. I pass them on to you— in tribute to her and her influence on me. I urge you to seek out her 1926 masterpiece, "Fairyland".

Ida, thank you for stoking my sense of wonder as a child, and for inspiring me as an artist later in life. You are well loved and well remembered.

"GARDEN OF DREAMS," BY IDA RENTOUL OUTHWAITE

1
— WRITE —
A POET ALL ALONG

I was a poet all along,
These letters must remind.
My muse amused— I am the song.
And choose my own in kind.

Once I'd begun to really doubt,
Eventually I said;
That he would make a poet out
Of anyone he wed.

'A lovely compliment.' said he,
My feather in his hat.
Another thing he stole from me,
Without a caveat.

But poets die and starve and groan,
To fill an empty space.
This hole inside, I carved alone.
I'll hold it now with grace.

A year's adage, an age, a youth,
I think, therefore I drown.
What thoughts will settle into truth,
If we don't write them down?

A day, a death. We lose ourselves,
Forgotten won't confer.
To stay the grim, this pen compels;
We wrote, therefore we were.

Such hopes, defeats, and desperate wants,
The pages set them free.
I never kept a journal once,
All this time— it's kept me.

An honest poem falls like a knife,
It hurts so good to catch.
So sweetly bliss is paired with strife,
Hence I'm a merry wretch.

I feel so sick, I'm filled with words,
They bubble from below.
I fear what might become of me,
I try to catch the flow.

I think I've been caught by a muse,
Her grip is like a vice.
For aching I am pulled from bed,
To write down her advice.

Is this the same that once besot,
My dear dead Emily?
For once prose came from careful thought,
And now it spills from me.

An ewer in Erato's hands,
Pours boiling to my head.
I'm burning while she makes demands,
'Amuse me now, instead.'

The emptiness I hold, my curse,
She's rending to fulfill.
By hearse or worse, each slender verse,
Is bending to her will.

To Calliope, I plead my case,
Still Erato responds.
'Your swells and aches, mark eros chase—
Shirk not when heart desponds.'

The sisters meet with Erato,
'Eldest, this one is mine.'
I can't deny her gifts bestow,
But still question the nine.

To Calliope, I bear it all—
Adventure, epics, tales!
But nine see me, the muses call;
'Your heart always prevails.'

To Erato, I bow my head—
'Why cry, my poiētēs?
To highs and lows, your passion's led,
By me you are most blessed.'

To Calliope, I seethe, I roar,
What love leaves legacy?
What import can love poems implore?
What mind unlocks this key?

To Erato, all credit due.
'Our only heirloom left.
Your mourning bells still ringing true;
Will guide a soul bereft.'

Who will I keep awake at night?
What mind might meet my own?
Hello? Through time, what glimpse of light,
Might I spark here alone?

At times it takes a hundred words,
Then tried a thousand ways.
To find a single truthful verse,
Whose meaning well conveys.

But when the rhymes come easily,
Beware as that is worse.
For not gets done by pageantry,
It's better to be terse.

How can I own a single word?
The ink and pen own me.
Who dares to own a hummingbird?
Enjoy them— let them be.

I've cast off all I left for worse,
Then walked the plank to ink.
Dove down through paper waves of verse,
And dared not stop to drink.

A poem composed— thus freshly pressed,
Like four leaf clover fold,
Might find and fend the one possessed,
To stave the gloaming's hold.

A poem might choke upon the noose,
My chalice overflows.
To gain all that I left to lose,
I swallow embryos.

Beware, you're not in on the joke.
Complicit in the crime.
Oh maiden, mother, crone— evoke.
The summit's still a climb.

Dear femmes— write true. Our future calls;
Compose or pass on late.
And when at last your feather falls,
Dried ink shall satiate.

In maiden white, with mother's ink,
What strength hath apron strings.
My plume is dripping, dare to drink?
I have no other springs.

A name holds power; et squelettes.
Qui est mon plume de nom?
If I was her, with no regrets,
To whom do I belong?

Oh patron of the bardic arts,
Come rhyme, come ride along.
Fly swan upon a breeze of hearts,
And barter hope for song.

Bring me a common garden poem,
With measured common sense.
Familiar lights the hearth at home,
Remember then, passed tense.

I've signed one name ten thousand times.
Been born then borne along.
If I could claim ten thousand names,
Then none could own my song.

And I, inherit or bequeath,
The heir and predecessor.
For back and forth, pawn turns to queen,
Both greater than and lesser.

The bloodless blush, the inky gore—
Behold mine brimming veins.
I am a writer, ever more.
This pen, syringe, ordains.

Release, be free mine nightingales,
In flight more sweetly sing—
Both words and birds wilt under veils,
I clip no paper wing!

My poems domestic, scattered, slight;
Quick dandelion seeds.
My voices quiet, late at night,
But planted grow like weeds.

Pull back these brittle tinder words,
How quickly fletch ignites.
Yes, these dried rhymes were sitting birds,
Released they light the nights.

My poems await, perched in the trees,
Foul-feathered, patience gone.
They roost on branches, brave the breeze,
But dare not fly til dawn.

"AND WEPT BITTERLY," BY IDA RENTOUL OUTHWAITE

2
— LATE —
WAYS TO LOSE

I fell for every courting dance,
He spun me round and round.
My shoes wore thin each second chance,
Till my feet touched the ground.

Magician on an empty stage,
Assistant, he's in need.
I volunteer, I chose my cage,
I trust the showman's lead.

Who does it all, behind the scenes?
I've made him look his best.
And when he smiles, by all means,
Do tell me I am blessed.

But there's no magic after all,
It's all just tricks, a ruse.
And I the fool, the duped and small,
Found one more way to lose.

I play pretend, a rotten start,
I mind no lie uncouth.
'Please champion your own damn heart.
Your body knows the truth.'

A bitter child's past upset,
That house of red and green.
Apologies will not abet,
And yet, what could have been.

Too long ago to be a crime.
Acknowledge to accuse.
A child gaslit into prime.
I dare not say   .

My oldest nemesis, hubris!
Still holding hands with doubt.
Their friendship baffles, so amiss.
Both cannot do without.

A kiss, a touch, our moon, our best;
The future— now our pasts.
Amidst those firsts I never guessed,
We'd so soon see our lasts.

So many many years ago;
I sowed a little seed.
Though our tree did not want to grow,
I paid it little heed.

Infertile field, I labored so!
I brought it better earth.
I prayed for sun, wished clouds to go;
Success pinned to my worth.

Then it grew quickly, towered up—
So many came to see.
I hid the rotting, twisted roots;
From everyone. But me.

Ten years today below white sky;
I watered every day.
And when we bloomed, I stopped to cry—
Our petals, withered, grey.

I cannot water any more.
Our roots shot shallow, old.
While you have lied upon the grass;
Our tree grew girdled, cold.

On far off hill, a tree once stood.
All grey from leaves to bark.
With no one left to care for it,
It choked out in the dark.

When I was young and foolish still,
A hopeful, tender green.
I met a careless man and fell.
He called himself a king.

Such honeyed words poured from his lips,
I hung on every word.
But he was cursed, so long ago
'Do nothing but be heard.'

He spoke of thrones, his vast kingdom,
Too soon we made a vow.
Us two to one, and one to none,
'I pledge myself to thou.'

With troth complete, I'd not foreseen,
That I'd be cursed then too.
For I was never once a queen,
But songbird, feathered through.

'Still cursed, am I.' He would lament,
'I can do not but beg.
But we can feast on words until,
You lay a golden egg.'

My feathered work, my gilded test,
Took years to carry out,
While he took pains in idle rest,
I brought the egg about.

He took it then, he took it all,
Named it his very own.
Told me to lay at beck and call;
Still left me all alone.

It was no use, to force a truce,
He'd nothing left to stake.
I'd always been his golden goose,
And that was my mistake.

His curse was sound, and spite it all,
His word was just a word.
With nothing left to keep me there,
I flew like any bird.

He spewed hot air, he raged and fought,
> But I took to the skies.
I've no time now, for what he's wrought,
> For petty kings and lies.

Proud lover thief, of lust, of fame,
'For us!' He cried, for one.
My worth a throne he sought to claim,
Till I left him with none.

'You're free,' he said. 'Do what you please.
Go be a shitty wife.
But if you ever try to leave,
I'll. Ruin. Your. Fucking. Life.'

And I in love, so breathless, hid.
I justified it all.
I think he saw before I did,
The writing on the wall.

So as I left, he banished me,
Sent riders who proclaimed,
That guilty now I planned to flee,
A bandit, felon, shamed.

So many folk believed his word,
I penned responses, framed.
His arrows shot down every bird,
And wholly I was blamed.

I ride at dusk, a dappled song,
Where are my merry men?
This end of wicks will not last long,
I must find hearth by then.

But when I knocked by candle light,
A friendly face denied.
The cold, the dark, this hardest night,
'I cannot pick a side.'

Imagine now your wasting groom,
A father then, instead.
You'll know the joy of barren wombs,
The comfort of the red.

My mother says she always knew;
I was a shooting star.
'He knew it too, saw all of you,
Thought you might take him far.'

My lover's friend warns him, explains;
'You better learn to fly.
She's learned to run with ball and chains,
She's headed for the sky.'

How can they both be so sincere,
My knees cave with a thud.
I cannot dream of clouds for fear,
I've landed in the mud.

The one who saw me to the bone,
I left him on that hill.
I once was loved and once was known.
I hope I can be still.

"SHE BEGAN TO CRY," BY IDA RENTOUL OUTHWAITE

3
— CHOICE —
DECAY OR RUNAWAY

For all those who once thought like me,
That you could make it right.
You're not alone, you'll never be,
This tunnel spills with light.

We hid amidst the roots and rock,
But sun's at either end.
Just pick a course and start to walk,
We'll find hope round the bend.

Beware— yet trudge that lantern on,
Let moths collect their due,
What light attracts will part come dawn,
But darkness might claim you.

I blew all of my wishes out.
But keep lit deep inside.
I feel the full forget me doubt,
But know my own damn mind.

Cold ego guards my wounded oath,
But hunger turns my pride.
I escape through the undergrowth,
Dread what I might not find.

These darkened woods do not keep thrones,
The dead cannot bend knees.
So feed the fire, warm your bones,
Let sparks fly past the trees.

Freedom or death, I burn white flags;
The bridges and the boats.
If courage or my campaign lags—
At least we're not turncoats.

We build the bite ablaze, bone fire,
Hope rising as white smoke.
Yes— toss your failures on the pyre,
We've nothing left to stoke.

I stop my ears and row each day,
One fear above crossbones.
My killer whale breaches to spray—
And drag me down to Jones.

I'm captain still, prow set towards land,
My ship cuts through the deep.
The wheel is bloody in my hands,
Been weeks since I could sleep.

A piercing song, a cry for aid;
There's someone drowning— there!
The same damn monster, grin betrayed,
I chant the skipper's prayer.

I've past the storms, the tossed shipwrecks,
Lost all my two-faced crew.
No captain could survive these decks,
I'm ready for the blue.

I'm in too deep to start to bail,
This gun is out of blanks.
Abandon ship. Naught to avail.
It's time I walked these planks.

My wings and tongue were never clipped—
    I seek that upper blue.
A siren's song or playwright's script,
    Hold nothing to the view.

Words flounder on my tongue, alone.
I must say 'I,' not 'we.'
Each sentence free, a milestone.
Not 'ours,' but 'mine.' Just me.

must write the script to toss it out
must have a mind to lose
must douse the skies to break the drought
must break my heart to choose

If all is fair in love, what's left?
A darling enemy.
If nothing's fair in love but theft,
What loot a heart might be.

Fly golden swan, you've found at last,
Cast off— your way to lose!
Goodbye bygones and feathered past,
Light is the life you choose.

A finger pointed at the tracks,
But I won't be compelled.
A finger pointed at the axe,
But I cannot be felled.

A road diverged in darkened wood,
The bayonets ahead.
Still frozen, shaking, there I stood,
A wake of mud and dread.

I took one salty look behind,
Pulled free, at last, turncoat.
How oft I opted to stay blind—
Leashed as a poor scapegoat.

Still patriot, I am somehow,
I've found my new homeland.
A traitor with a broken vow,
Can still offer a hand.

Whoa— steady now, black brim, no spurs,
 No sheriff's star to doubt.
I've ridden off and left what's yers,
 No heed, no last shoot out.

False pride cost you that swindler's hat,
A sham of ivory.
No town was ever worth all that.
You've seen the last of me.

Dim mirrors, pity, woe's trespass,
And Heaven's boiled stars.
A shattered home of fine stained glass.
All counted in my scars.

My teapot brimmed with heartache melts,
To gladness on my tongue.
But tea will steep to bitterness,
If it is brewed too long.

I pick my scabs on sorry days,
Still parched after the flood.
He never laid a hand on me,
So why then so much blood?

My heart yet sick, veins thick with mud,
The witch doctor will try.
At last I dare to let this blood;
With leaches, my ally.

If no one feeds the pigeons then?
Where will they dare to fly?
Will I survive on smidgens thin?
Or bid it all goodbye?

I'm going through a lot these days,
Home broken feeling mute.
The point is not to solve the maze,
But find joy while en route.

Mud cannot rob you of your name,
Chains cannot hold your mind.
To flee: leave care. abandon blame.
You must be stronger spined.

Now eat the apples, climb the tree.
Chew truth and feel the cold.
To know the garden, choose to flee—
Cast out? That's what we're told.

Those half healed hurts you drag along—
The scars, the pain, the fear.
Let space and grace eclipse their song,
Choose well what you revere.

I broke the spell of hazel rings,
That lined a stump of grey.
No net can catch my golden wings,
The one that got away.

So many people had it worse,
Not right's not always wrong.
Comparison's a gentle nurse,
She's why I stayed so long.

If only I could drink the moon,
She pairs well with regret.
For I'll have none and plenty soon,
To sip till I forget.

He thought he'd never have to stop,
He hoped it was a bluff.
He tried to keep me all locked up;
No tower's tall enough.

And I, the monster, now depart.
The villain in his lie.
He speaks of my capricious heart,
But can't ask himself why.

I do not want to be a guide.
I do not want to fail.
I do not want to waste or bide.
Yet heartstrings still prevail.

The waves and long experience,
Have sunk a ship below.
Mourn not this craft of Theseus,
We lost ours long ago.

If times are bad in good times too,
Seek higher ground than haze.
In clearer air, take in the view,
To break free from the maze.

I peeled the shadows from my soles.
Then set the darkness free.
Those footprints left are empty holes,
None dare to follow me.

I'll bloom again, a new encore,
With petals crystal clear.
I purged the thorn and soil floor,
I'm gone and finally here.

"...THE FAIRY QUEEN," BY IDA RENTOUL OUTHWAITE

4
— REBIRTH —
I SEE BY HEART

Red shadows spun on walls, insides,
And I, canary, knew.
His mouth, his lies. My heart, misguides.
On time and overdue.

I heard her song, still underground,
  But freedom looked like woe.
The golden wood above uncrowned.
  I doubted, dusk below.

'See with your soul— not eyes, my dear.
This darkness is a ruse.
Where is your lionhearted cheer?
What more have you to lose?'

By answer I plucked wings and dare,
I flew from crypt to light.
Then dazed I saw a lady there,
My fate survived the night.

'I know your name, your love, your vice.
My pupil, from today.'
Then she cut clean through both my eyes.
'Those gifts often betray.'

Now all I see, I see by heart,
I'm gleaming, gilded, grown.
Behold, the world is so like art,
Unknowable and known.

Misfortune bestows boons as well—
Beware life lived without.
To never taste your potential,
Choose leisure over doubt.

All walk atop life's sharpened edge,
To fall on either side.
Sweet softened feet upon that ledge,
Might gash if long you bide.

A lifetime's not a legacy,
Best sow your nows with care,
The fog of fate bounds what we see,
But hearts grow everywhere.

I doused my temper, let it cool,
Disarmed myself, delayed.
'Be worthy of the Fury, fool;
Forge back your plow to blade.'

Your candle's lit, one spark of fate,
Each hour chews the wick.
So bask in warmth, delight, create—
A joyful life's not quick.

In earshot of my woe Madam,
In manner of the fen.
Content I was, content I am,
Content I'll be again.

'You snub my gift with each display.
Now hark your own demands.
My harvest of a grain each day,
You turn them to commands.'

'Be still. A heart cannot heal fast.
Observe mine shifting hands.
A changing mind whose growth will last,
Must swim a tide of sands.'

'You falter in the waves, my dear.
Do not then chide defeat.
Be gentle first, and self revere.
Each time you fall, be sweet.'

My mistress time, my muse, my sign,
How best to wield your gift?
No pity for a weakened spine—
Her hands are wont to drift.

'Why do you count the minutes, lass?
I tallied yours to reap.
What waste to watch the hourglass—
They are not yours to keep.'

Until the moon herself flew down,
I'd lost my way, my care.
'Do take my hand, before you drown.'
I saw her standing there.

My mistress keeps her careful hands,
On faces and on glass.
She measures memories out in sands,
Marks moments as they pass.

Not long ago, I lay preserved,
Felt dread at every dawn.
I thought time frozen, unobserved,
And life itself withdrawn.

Yet still she counts, and I had fled—
    Hid even from the sun.
I veiled her face, I joined the dead,
    Refused to hear her song.

It's hard to live amongst the dead.
They whisper from the black,
'To save yourself, don't look ahead,
Stay still upon your back.'

'...this is the best you'll ever be...'
I'm wrapped in cotton, white.
But wait... but wait. This is not me.
Her sands were always bright.

The slab is heavy on my tomb,
I lift it all the same.
I am not dead! I cry, I croon,
I don't know my own name.

Her hands are moving me again,
As if she always knew.
I'll never die again, my pen,
We must keep moving too.

No rock fears cutting wind or rain,
No tree fears fallen leaves.
No storm fears sun or weather vane.
No heart fears pins or sleeves.

'Sleep with the sun, not moon, my dear.
Save starlight for Beltane.
A debt of sand is one to fear,
Best pay your tax in grain.'

Medusa's power's in her laugh,
Her will to carry on.
Who dares to speak on her behalf?
Defy till denouement.

'Now practice, dear, read twixt the lines,
Sweet time trims on each face.
Fork foe from friend, and learn the signs.
Keen trust sharpens your grace.'

'Foul weather friends shout back the storms—
Fight on through wind and rain.
Each thunderclap and squall confirm;
Rejoice. The true remain.'

'Behold the past only and if,
The viewing pleases you.
Take in old sights, but mind the cliff,
Direct fresh eyes to blue.'

The heart may choose, the mind wants more,
One heals the other counts.
But neither knows what to ask for,
And both have lost accounts.

From me to me, and I to I,
We see what bowed our brow.
The past is lost; at last gone by—
I can forgive me now.

"CASTAWAY," BY IDA RENTOUL OUTHWAITE

5
— LOST —
CURSED AND CLOSED

Believe, breathe deep, you are a rock,
All grey and white, a bore.
Tides rise and fall beneath the dock—
But you are on the shore.

I dare not knock on other doors,
Or sort my friends from foes.
But those who idle through your wars,
Are tallied in your woes.

Beware the men with endless lungs,
All crocodile eyed.
Beware encrusted silver tongues,
Who've never tasted pride.

Return the joy I lent you, please,
Those splinters of my heart.
With you, a gouge each time you squeeze,
With me, mosaic art.

Should I confess, to break my peace—
And speak against this man?
To arm the world, with truth at least,
How can I let things stand?

I cannot warn or arm them all,
nor save a single heart.
I could not break my own damn fall,
nor speedily depart.

He cannot aim at silent rocks,
Cannot engage with nix,
Pandora warns, my own voice box,
Might spawn more hurt than fix.

The shameful shovel blame by hand,
That labor leaves a trace.
If temper tempts, do no grand stand,
Keep clean hands gloved, in grace.

The stories that we tell ourselves,
Swell taller than the truth.
Outgrow your skin to deeper delve,
Shed flesh for claw and tooth.

Towards certain things I'm still afraid,
Yet not for coward's pride.
I know not how to ask for aid,
Nor invite help inside.

'How can you let such slander stand?
They storm the gates— the wall!'
My crumbled castle left unmanned?
No one will hear it fall.

When my voice fails, and too my pen,
Why must I let lies lie?
To swallow poison, once again...
At times I'd rather die.

Since candid is the road love paves,
Be known and know complete.
The cobblestones of friendship graves,
Lie down a gated street.

An alley fenced in pearly white,
Cool sun feigned in the gloom.
The tenants seize each ghostly slight,
Intent to worst assume.

A seeming lane so kept and fine,
All rosy, not to fret!
The curtains veil a hidden shrine,
Of envy and regret.

Her painted porcelain complains,
No callers anymore.
Friends stroll on by her window panes;
Tis she who locked the door.

Embrace the tide and ride along,
Sprout fins and gills and tail.
If you're to sing a siren's song,
Enthrall them all— prevail!

To friends of envy, bid adieu,
Some things you cannot teach.
If you're to laugh at insults too,
Best first get out of reach.

I've not to do with petty minds,
Assume and guess the worst.
I cannot speak at all, I find,
For fear of being cursed.

You'll tie a ribbon, wrap in haste,
Light candles just to blow.
Please mind your pride is never laced;
Such gifts aren't worth the bow.

How tempting tis, to test your might,
To pull a sword from stone.
Someday you'll face a worthy fight,
Till then leave graves alone.

Accept no millstone as a gift,
Nor carry guilt around.
Why bear a weight you cannot lift?
Leave folly on the ground.

Farewell false friends with all to prove,
Each thought so bitter fought.
Befoed by all, yet never move,
Your proof is ever naught.

Swept underneath this tattered rug,
I lived in darkened dust.
With justice lost and tunnel dug—
My freedom springs from trust.

I look for meaty things to bite.
The moon is on my side.
I sit, I seethe, I chew, I fight,
But feed no wolves inside.

The sirens sing the sailors down,
A grave for every liar.
But honest lovers seldom drown,
More often join the choir.

Lemons they give! And little aid!
Expecting all returns.
But you owe no one lemonade,
Take care, this table turns.

For plenty peace breeds cowards all;
Who can't afford to choose.
Yet hardship, strain— the bold grow tall,
With nothing left to lose.

Oh, if I ever break the rules,
I'll do so with intent.
Since brimming heaven takes no fools,
Best put off my ascent.

To vanquish dragons, train your own.
Know when to fly or fight.
Learn how to sit upon your throne.
A balanced crown is light.

When saneness lies, and madness stands,
Ungloved candor; uncouth.
In life at times you'll shake both hands,
And there you'll glimpse the truth.

Good pardon me, my drifting friend,
Not every day goes well.
My eyes at least cannot amend,
But unseen? That is hell.

Oh kith and kin, like a disease,
From poor to very rich!
To start a family is but ease—
To keep one is the hitch.

Each feeling like an insect, pinned.
Now stuck and studied, claimed.
No moth or butterfly on wind.
They cannot flutter framed.

Treading, trodden, tout forgotten,
I'm out of rhythm now.
Weathered wood— preserved or rotten,
Still sweat sold off my brow.

My heart and mind forgot to judge,
So no one's keeping score.
If one should choose, and one begrudge;
I don't know anymore.

At present I am safe and sound,
It's well you've asked at last.
So many missing, lost then found;
Now that the worst is past.

"...TO AND FRO," BY IDA RENTOUL OUTHWAITE

6
— CHANCE —
FLUSH OF HEART

was this a garden long ago
is something hidden here
the paths are forked obscured in snow
we all could disappear

and am I chasing being chased
amidst forgotten trees
our feet find paths of chance in haste
a cat before us flees

if merry meet and merry part,
    I'll sing our song til then.
if we can tarry in these woods,
    I'll never leave again.

Yes, you can pen your music scores,
Then play your solo sets,
Compose a song that's purely yours;
But Chance prefers duets.

Smitten, to smite, a fitting phrase.
Love strikes like lightning rods.
Count seconds twixt that thunder haze;
Best first forget the odds.

what is this light between the firs
this feeling in our bones
even the night around us yearns
we dance over the stones

The road is gone, the air is cold,
we shiver in the dark.
Our rays of sun so tender now,
enough to make their mark.

if winter comes and winter goes
I'll still enjoy the view
and if this sleeping garden grows
I'll spend my springs with you

Oh! With such ease, these bare hands bruise,
Affection's like a glove.
As like to fit as it's to lose,
I'm nervous now, in love.

A morning fresh, past blankets, dew,
a sip of golden blend.
If dawn can hope and love renew,
how can she bear to end?

I fear I love too much too soon,
At once wound tight and slack.
I melt each languid afternoon,
Can't hold you and hold back.

this way perhaps, or is it there
we pause as if we're close
this frigid air, a cold snaps snare
has crept up to our toes

it's hard to tell just where we've been
now that we've stopped to see
we're wrapped in why's and how's and when's
feel bound and boundless— free

On beaten hearts off beaten paths,
One riddle left to lose.
A little lost, a little found,
Yet still we get to choose.

Find feline sense of dare and space,
Reach treetop winds and view—
To make real magic commonplace,
The words are: I love you.

My gentle brewer tamps and knocks,
From course to fine and back.
He'll steal the crown from Goldilocks,
Then pen an almanac.

Come love, take heart, our garden grows,
Towards heaven into earth.
We shape and pluck what nature sows,
Yet know not what its worth.

Recall those rosy envelopes?
Amidst the ice and cold?
Soft wishes we've sown into hopes,
Kept warm in our handhold.

Past winter fell and autumn chaste,
From foraged spring anew;
Our flowered fruit with summer haste,
Grew bountied trust from few.

Watch quick— our wistful garden grows!
The frost at last withdrawn.
Let's cherish vines and moss and crows,
And meet at every dawn.

My frozen bones to flame flecked stones,
Suns set and mountains rise.
A season scooped in ice cream cones,
Your dimples the reprise.

Two odds add up to even out,
To play, to get, to chase,
Since Chance found us, I've little doubt,
Her bet's already placed.

A first of happy birthdays, love,
The hourglass refrain,
No poem could ever say enough—
I cherish every grain.

Us two of swords, the hangman's game;
Cards dealt just as they lay.
The shuffle of our lives became,
A lucky hand to play.

Our chips all in, and I believe,
Fate's stacked our deck to start.
Still I've kept something up my sleeve;
A royal flush of heart.

You've shown your hand— upon your knee!
Another candle lit.
You've made a gambler out of me.
And us? The winning bet.

Make now so many hopeful vows;
Yet keep one for your own.
A promise first to self espouse,
With heart and heartache shown.

To you— keep true, then consort too.
When worse or better brings.
Go gather rosebuds, mind the view;
Find strength in tied heart strings.

A year ago, or more or less,
We chased a gilded glade.
For then and now and further— yes.
My ringing answer made.

How fast our darkest clouds skip by,
Your hammock twixt the trees.
How free our days of purple sky,
Us climbing through the breeze.

I dream of golden mornings soft
drawn curtains, gleaming rays
our handprints gild the dust aloft
in early hour glaze

I dream of days with you most oft
across the pond to greys
with golden rings we hold, our croft,
to last us all our days

It marks us now— in truth, true love,
Must end in tragedy.
One parts, one bides, a mourning dove,
Regret not bended knee.

The happy endings— fairytales.
They finish, all the same.
Delight in middles, love prevails,
Beginnings overcame.

Goodnight my darling, fare thee well,
An honor it has been.
One day we'll hear that bitter bell—
Yet choose our path again.

"ECHO," BY IDA RENTOUL OUTHWAITE

7
— DREAM —
CALL THE FAIRIES

Alas, the only Magic left,
Lives on past whimsy road.
The wistful, hopeful, and bereft,
Might visit her abode.

If once you knew the woodland words,
  Yet lost your mother tongue,
Hark new again to dawn songbirds,
  Be twice— both old and young.

If you can dance a ring of air,
Round compasses and trees,
Drink deep the earth and hum a prayer,
To flowers like the bees.

If you can call the fairies still,
Blow kisses to the moon,
Accompany the whip-poor-will,
Drink deep the rains of June.

If you can breathe horizons in,
Hold sunsets in your chest,
Exhale the doubts and fog within,
And sing while still at rest.

Then one day you may love again,
Be blissful, bitter free.
Find magic like a sigh within,
And promised, there I'll be.

Into the woods, away from kings,
New friends at last are found.
Our fire lit with bare heartstrings,
We gather close around.

Make friends of ardor and mundane,
Trail roots while yet you roam.
Mix common with the high arcane,
And both will point you home.

If home is where you hang your hat,
You must first put it on.
Go toil, tug, and trim the fat,
A home's worth more when won.

A house of rosy-tinted-glass;
As brittle as thin ice.
A crystal home cannot surpass,s
A hidden paradise.

Our new abode, no guarantees;
A promise built in brick.
We'll fill it full of memories,
Yet never be homesick.

We'll follow wind and whim, blue jay,
Then roost in our own nest.
We'll see the world! We'll fly away!
Then wing back home to rest.

All migratory birds agree,
They know the way by heart.
Homecoming to their favorite tree,
Sweetens the time apart.

Find safety in the numbered crowd,
With many friendly eyes.
Where even children are allowed,
To venture past moonrise.

Rainbows return on winter's breast,
Rejoice in slanted rays,
Let's bathe in color, stop to rest,
And never count the days.

The mountains worry they are late
The flowers they postpone
This rocky spring of ours can wait
Til hummingbirds fly home.

This dart awaits a map unfurled,
Throw caution down the road.
We'll dance upon this spinning world—
Your handhold my abode.

Our lady teases paramours,
As love is easy caught.
Take care to stoke it out of doors,
Fair Fortune shrinks from naught.

Go do your good deeds on the road,
What weight light acts might ease!
Yet never tally what you're owed;
The doing must appease.

Let sail our hearts through sunny storms,
Through wind and haze and night.
Once all was rocky, shapeless forms—
Soon hindsight will delight.

Oh, someone moved my cheese. And then!
Another got my goat.
And whose to blame, time and again?
Tis I, the casting vote.

Do misconduct! It's all witch hunts;
The rare fare well behaved.
A wasted wanted truth wont fronts,
Spend life— none can be saved.

I savor oranges once again,
And fresh pineapples too.
If citrus sours, now and then,
I'll lay blame where its due.

My mind and heart ran off, eloped,
They dance in mirrored stride.
Nothing has gone just as I hoped,
But life's a wild ride.

Just you and me, with quest in hand.
A single stitch to start.
Our heartstrings weave a new homeland,
A tapestry of heart.

I dream again, as time returns,
In promised wonderland,
Two red and heavy hummingbirds,
Alight on either hand.

I take my mountains where I go.
They raised me wild-willed.
In flattened lands, in fields below,
Past roots are mine instilled.

"...SCATTERING STARS," BY IDA RENTOUL OUTHWAITE

8
— HOPE —
COURAGE CATCHES

Their fear might be contagious, yes.
But courage catches too.
No cure to madness yet, unless,
A braver soul stays true.

My shape a square, my path a hole—
I'll breakdown to breakthrough.
In pieces past, my summoned soul,
Might forge my form anew.

I saw the flash of mountain top,
Struck lightning through the gloom.
The road is rough, the rain won't stop—
But heartache's our heirloom.

This mountain must be climbed while blind,
Storm veiled from hill to hill.
Just hold the peak inside your mind,
And seek that summit still.

'Go find yourself!' A fool's advice.
As if you're lost out there.
Outrun yourself to paradise?
Alas, you're everywhere.

Not I, then who? Not now, then when?
I'll stoke my care within.
I'm here, I'm through. I know, I've been.
I'll not standby again.

Up Sanitas, us seekers seek,
To climb its noble heights.
The quest for grail at yonder peak,
Turns cowards into knights.

First temperament, grow sound your mind,
Pick course and carry on.
Take care to choose a worthy guide,
And pace yourself through dawn.

Next brawn and might must forge a way,
Then tread it through the night.
On any path, in any fray—
Keep strength or lose the fight.

The final test, the last summit,
A riddle for the wise:
What songbird caged can still plummet,
Will soar but never flies?

If you're to don the armor soon,
Where is your drum of war?
What chest contains the greatest boon?
What would you dare die for?

Take heart; my loves, past timberlines,
The good and true break through.
On Sanitas your virtue shines,
The grail is gone— pursue!

Our clouds shine silver, thunder past,
Their linings black, bygone.
We've overcome, we'll live the last!
Our luck's arrived— hang on.

Toss seeds to wayward winds and wait,
Count losses with your wins.
Do find a funny friend in fate,
Don't end where chance begins.

Oh please don't let your nerves delay,
A gesture of goodwill.
A call, a wish, a small bouquet,
Will ease a climb uphill.

Be good and true and beautiful.
Mind not observer's eye.
Be self and selfless, dutiful,
Let love and logic try.

A master first of self, of mind;
In times of dearth and wealth.
A stoic joy, if you remind,
And don't hinder yourself.

You are the damsel and the knight,
Wear steel over your lace.
Though thorns may catch and rust may bite,
Fight on with sword and grace.

A sunny disposition shrouds,
The foggiest forecast.
Still I cannot control the clouds;
The rains will come— then pass.

The wise advise some little lies;
A tit for tat plus one.
For smiles spent on passerbys,
Aren't lost as much as won.

A flaunted bloom will wilt too soon,
Of envy withered roots.
In secret gardens, water, prune;
Then taste your ripened fruits.

A pretty flower braves the vase,
    Is fame worth such a cut?
Both tame or wild wilt apace—
Choose gardener's knife or rut.

When even peace sows cunning fears,
What hope have we of rest?
Wield watering can and pruning sheers—
Weeds grow at your behest.

Foremost, you must befriend your soul.
Cast off loathing to soothe.
Then quiet sit, alone, console,
Recall your inner truth.

You'll wield the needle and the knife,
You'll sow as much as raze.
You'll wonder— save, or spend a life?
You'll reap both blame and praise.

Beware false idols, guard your hearts.
Vain worship will confuse.
The late and myth: both finer starts.
Choose carefully your muse.

An idle hand's a devil's tool.
No sweat to balance bliss.
A craftsman or a softened fool—
Which will you reminisce?

My lips, a guard, no careless prose;
No lashing tête-à-tête.
Keep silver tongues behind teeth closed—
Or live to taste regret.

No freedom is perennial,
Go gather last year's seeds.
Each spring prepare their burial,
Or next year harvest weeds.

An amateur might practice on,
Until it is done right.
But watch, true masters carry on,
Till failure's in hindsight.

What force kills courage, routs the knights,
Halts birdsong and stops tracks?
The Unknown feeds those pitied frights,
Reveals inside what lacks.

Take care, dear crowns, of apathy.
Indifference will corrode.
To care once more, to flee ennui,
Set feet upon the road.

Be brave, dear crowns, let banners fly,
Mind not the circling crows.
To mend your will, do not stand by,
A lack of courage grows.

"FAIRY OF THE SNOW," BY IDA RENTOUL OUTHWAITE

9
— AGE —
TIMELESS TIMED

Oh I am woman, timeless timed,
I move and do not count.
My minutes? Motions. Hours? Climbed.
In mountains I surmount.

In times of shame and guilt, have grace.
For hope, believe in truth.
If you are blamed and scorned, embrace.
And envy not the youth.

Wear rosy wrinkles on your cheeks,
Cast wishes on sunk stones.
Remember what your brave heart seeks,
Let age embold your bones.

My friends are late, so often passed,
I meet them on the page.
Their souls preserved in books, steadfast.
Yet ever of the age.

Good stories earn their bindings, prose,
Each page turns in a blink.
A bliss filled life, as Morgan knows,
May not be worth the ink.

Time will repeat that old wive's tale,
Come maiden, mother, crone.
To have your choice of holy grail,
You cannot walk alone.

Death's frozen scales find no difference,
In high or low beneath.
Unfairly borne end squarely hence,
And ashes all bequeath.

Make friends again with destiny,
One bee cannot be great.
Each meets with dear mortality,
Yet new blooms do not wait.

The wind will blow, the young brought low,
King Holly does his worst.
Yet time bestows, the elder knows—
Spring follows winter first.

A rusty blade's not trusty aid,
And withered brawn's not strong.
In rain or shine, less talent fade—
Trudge true, and practice on.

Forget-me-not or lily wreathes.
We cannot choose our shroud.
Some die on pedestals as thieves,
Then later lose the crowd.

You are a human, not a god.
With mortal blood and bone.
Ignoble chase that void facade.
The deathless can't atone.

Behave as though one foot is plunged,
Already in your grave.
One blink until your light's expunged—
Keep on. You cannot save.

So swallow back those shredding words,
Choose well your deeds and friends.
Discard your worries, feed the birds—
Live well until it ends.

The odd or ordinary strife—
We never had much say.
If you were born into this life,
Then you're allowed to stay.

Will grief and joy arrive on time?
More often lost or late.
With grace, let pass the dear clock's chime,
Your heart heeds not the date.

If hardness ever hardiness,
Is mother to us all—
How slowly maturation sets,
Without hardship to call.

How oft a frame destroys the slate,
It does no good to rush.
No painting's ever done, so wait.
You do not hold the brush.

My needle pulls the thread of me,
Each day one stitch, one try.
I'll weave a worthy tapestry,
No day will pass me by.

Why wait! Why wait! The flowers cry;
Could patience go to seed?
'I'm late! I'm late!' A rabbit's lie—
Our fate's a scrappy weed.

The glaciers weep themselves away,
How quiet are their cries.
The lost await come yesterday,
We're left to eulogize.

Retreat inside still winter's womb.
Root deep to bide the sting.
A flower knows she's not entombed,
And hibernates till spring.

Be bold. But look, one less is more.
Be fine. Yet do not jeer.
Be hard. And lovely, either, or.
Be coy. But speak up, dear!

Beware the thrill of worldly things;
The dead cannot possess.
We only keep our spun heartstrings,
Enjoy, yet spurn excess.

'Pry open that old locket, Rook,
A heart thrives in full sun.
Pin hope again to sleeves and look—
Our best is oft homespun.'

Before and after, philos wills,
The daily doing same.
When living lacks, intention fills,
What changes is the frame.

A rot of undead hours spent;
As ghosts of future past.
Still wonder where your lifetime went?
Present yourself at last.

How long or little life will take,
Does nature not disdain?
Bear present time for it's own sake,
Bent not towards future gain.

A shoddy ship sinks in the storm.
Forgotten gardens wilt.
Repair your bridges while its warm,
Or lose what once you built.

The rotten old facade their fear.
Disguised as painted youth.
Are wrinkles not a blessing dear?
Do not hide from the truth.

To you, a happy birthday yet,
To you, a purple dawn.
To you, a year without regret,
To you, a life kept on.

Oh friend, oh dearest friend of mine.
Just how were we to know?
Our friendship just a little vine,
We'd bloom but not outgrow.

How far its spread, all on its own,
Without much time to tend.
Those little seeds we scattered, sown,
Might last until the end.

We're both so very far away,
Look at our garden now.
The brambles, brush, we'll clear some day,
I solemnly avow.

What secrets will the future hold,
What warmth and bitter cold?
What gift is hindsight for the bold,
What fortune for the old.

POSTFACE.

Thank you for joining me on this journey through three years of joy and heartache.

Merry met, to all of you who have tread these woods before and may do so again. Let us keep our lanterns lit, and seek out those twinkling lights in the distance.

Divergent folk, survivors, the clinically creative— I am comforted in knowing so many of us persevere, scattered quietly all over the world, lighting up the paths for one another.

I hope these poems find hearths and homes, and I thank all of you who help them find their way.

ACKNOWLEDGMENTS.

Alone I wrote this book of poems; yet love and generosity from many saw it published.

To all who took a chance to help my words find light at last; thank you. I hope one of these many poems finds a home in you.

To all the adventurous folk who joined the kickstarter; thank you. Your love drowns my doubt. I will remember you, always.

To all who find and spread this book, in far flung future days; you keep these paper birds in flight, and have my thanks always.

And to my love, my cats, my found and forged families; I love you, no poem could ever say enough.

ABOUT THE POET.

I grew up in the high rockies of Colorado, and reside now along her foothills. Words, and their arrangement into poems, have fascinated me since I was toddling. Homecoming to poetry in my late twenties was more compulsion than choice.

I began writing to make sense of abuse, divorce, ostracism, injuries, surgery, and recovery; mental and physical. My pen and I persisted, as stubborn as ever. I was a strong willed child too, a blessing which still helps me to handle dyslexia, ocd, adhd, and a connective tissue disorder. I hope sharing will help inspire others to do the same. Page 20, please write!

If the rest of this book is not enough about me, you may find more on my website:
WWW.AIMEEWOODWORKS.COM

OTHER BOOKS AND EDITIONS.

MERRY MEET & MERRY PART EDITIONS.

Paperback Heartache Edition
Hardcover Collector's Heirloom Edition
Audiobook and Digital Editions
Watercolor Art Prints of Select Poetry

OTHER WORKS BY AIMEE WOOD.

The Unofficial Legend of Zelda Cookbook

FIND THESE AND MORE AT:
www.aimeewoodworks.com

www.ingramcontent.com/pod-product-compliance
Lightning Source LLC
Chambersburg PA
CBHW060548080526
44585CB00013B/490